Master Maths at Home

Graphs and Measuring

Scan the QR code to help your child's learning at home.

 DK | **MATHS** NO PROBLEM!

mastermathsathome.com

How to use this book

Maths — No Problem! created Master Maths at Home to help children develop fluency in the subject and a rich understanding of core concepts.

Key features of the Master Maths at Home books include:

- Carefully designed lessons that provide structure, but also allow flexibility in how they're used.

- Speech bubbles containing content designed to spark diverse conversations, with many discussion points that don't have obvious 'right' or 'wrong' answers.

- Rich illustrations that will guide children to a discussion of shapes and units of measurement, allowing them to make connections to the wider world around them.

- Exercises that allow a flexible approach and can be adapted to suit any child's cognitive or functional ability.

- Clearly laid-out pages that encourage children to practise a range of higher-order skills.

- A community of friendly and relatable characters who introduce each lesson and come along as your child progresses through the series.

You can see more guidance on how to use these books at **mastermathsathome.com**.

We're excited to share all the ways you can learn maths!

Copyright © 2022 Maths — No Problem!

Maths — No Problem!
mastermathsathome.com
www.mathsnoproblem.com
hello@mathsnoproblem.com

First published in Great Britain in 2022 by
Dorling Kindersley Limited
One Embassy Gardens, 8 Viaduct Gardens, London SW11 7BW
A Penguin Random House Company

The authorised representative in the EEA is Dorling Kindersley
Verlag GmbH. Amulfstr. 124, 80636 Munich, Germany

10 9 8 7 6 5 4 3 2 1
001-327091-Jan/22

A CIP catalogue record for this book is available from the British Library.

ISBN: 978-0-24153-936-1
Printed and bound in the UK

For the curious
www.dk.com

This book was made with Forest Stewardship Council™ certified paper – one small step in DK's commitment to a sustainable future. For more information go to www. dk.com/our-green-pledge

Acknowledgements
The publisher would like to thank the authors and consultants Andy Psarianos, Judy Hornigold, Adam Gifford and Dr Anne Hermanson.

The Castledown typeface has been used with permission from the Colophon Foundry.

Contents

Ruby Elliott Amira Charles Lulu Sam Oak Holly Ravi Emma Jacob Hannah

Drawing and reading pictograms

The pictogram shows the favourite sport of each pupil in Class 4A.
Each pupil chooses one sport.
What information can you get from the pictogram?

Favourite Sport of Pupils in Class 4A

basketball	netball	cricket	tennis	football

Each ball stands for one pupil.

Example

There are 34 pupils in Class 4A.
The most popular sport is football.
Ten pupils choose football as their favourite sport.

$4 + 8 + 7 + 5 + 10 = 34$

The least popular sport is basketball.
Only 4 pupils choose basketball as their favourite sport.
Six more pupils choose football than choose basketball.

$10 - 4 = 6$

This pictogram shows the flavour of ice cream children in Year 2 chose as their favourite.

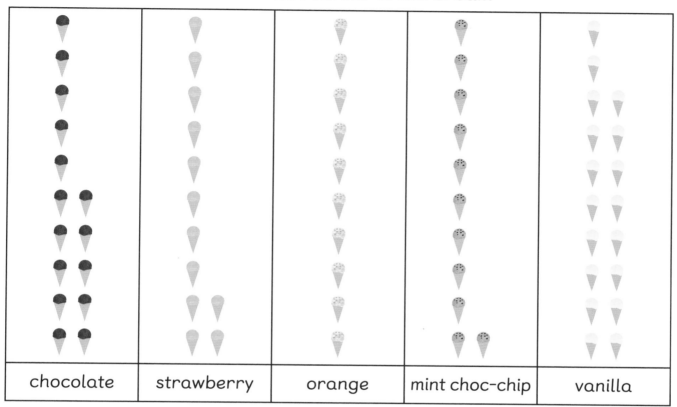

Favourite Flavour of Ice Cream

| chocolate | strawberry | orange | mint choc-chip | vanilla |

Each cone stands for one child.

1 Put the ice cream flavours in order from the least popular to the most popular.

| | | | | |

2 Fill in the blanks.

(a) [ ] more children chose chocolate ice cream than chose strawberry ice cream.

(b) Two fewer children chose [ ] ice cream than chose [ ] ice cream.

Drawing and reading bar graphs

Starter

This table shows the favourite pet of each pupil in Year 4. How can we show this information as a graph?

Favourite Type of Pet in Year 4

Pet	dog	fish	cat	rabbit	hamster
Number of pupils	36	12	58	34	24

Example

This is a **bar graph.**

Bar graphs are good for comparing information.

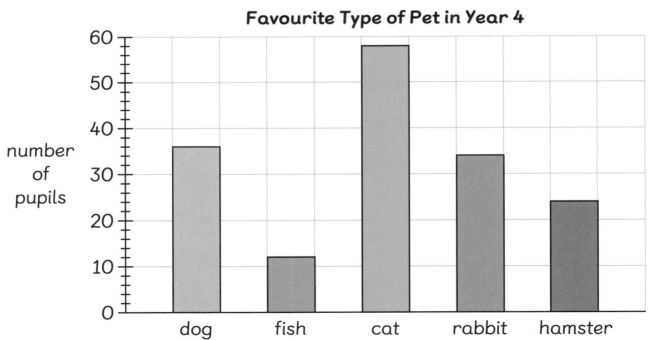

We can show this information on a bar graph.

1   A group of children were asked what their favourite meal is.
     Their answers are in the table.

Favourite Meal

Meal	burger and chips	roast chicken	ham salad	pizza	fish pie
Number of children	26	18	12	34	22

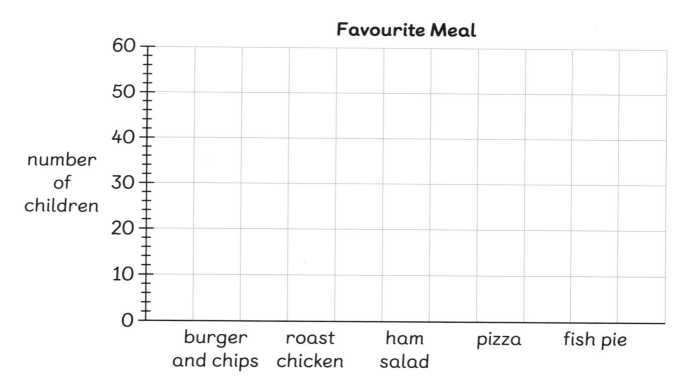

Favourite Meal

Draw bars on the graph to show the information in the table.

Among the group of children, [ ] is the most popular

meal and [ ] is the least popular meal.

Reading line graphs

Starter

Charles recorded the temperature in the school playground at different times in one day.

Time	09:00	10:00	11:00	12:00	13:00	14:00	15:00	16:00
°C	15	16	18	20	23	25	25	22

How can we show this information on a graph?

Example

This is called a **line graph**.

A line graph shows how things change really well.

Temperature in the School Playground

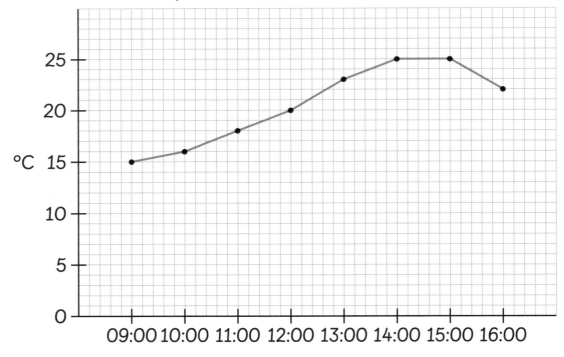

I can see when the temperature was at its highest and how quickly it changed.

We can use a line graph to show the information.

The line graph shows the average monthly rainfall in London.

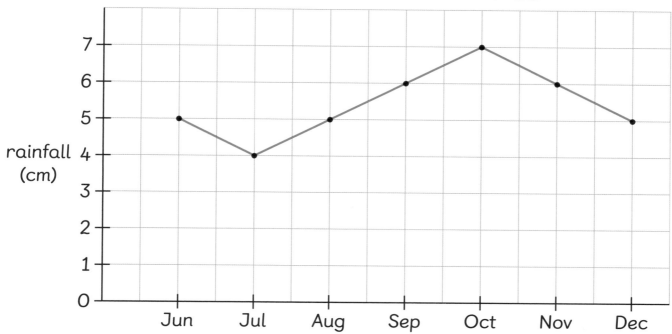

Rainfall in London Over 7 Months

1. Which month had the highest amount of rainfall?

2. Which month had the least amount of rainfall?

3. How many months had an average rainfall of 5 cm?

4. By how much did the average rainfall increase between July and September?   cm

5. By how much did the average rainfall decrease between October and December?   cm

6.   and   both had 6 cm of rainfall during the 7-month period.

Drawing line graphs

Oak is doing a project for her class on the rising prices for swimming. She made this table to show the changing prices at a water park over 6 years.

Year	Ticket Price
2014	£3.00
2015	£3.60
2016	£4.20
2017	£5.00
2018	£6.40
2019	£8.00

What types of graphs can Oak use to show this information?

Example

I think Oak should use a bar graph. Bar graphs are good for comparing things.

I think she should try both ways.

A line graph might be better. She wants to show how quickly the price has changed.

I can see the price for each year on the bar graph. It's easy to compare one bar to another.

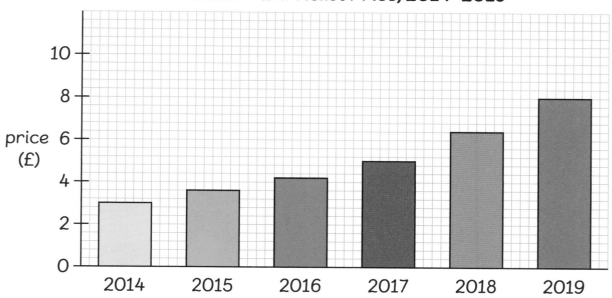

Water Park Ticket Price, 2014–2019

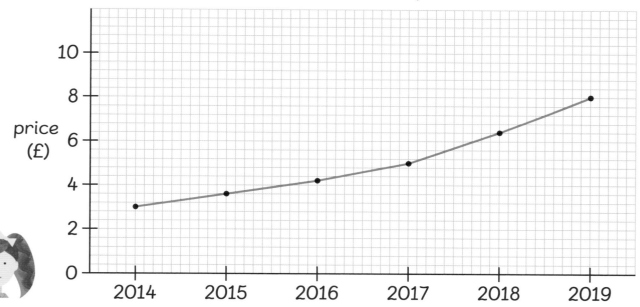

Water Park Ticket Price, 2014–2019

The line graph shows me how quickly the price changed really well.

When we use a line graph to show how something changes over time we can also call it a **time graph**.

Oak should use a line graph for her project.

1 The table shows the different prices for a holiday cottage over a period of 8 months.

Draw a line graph using the information in the table.

Month	Apr	May	Jun	Jul	Aug	Sep	Oct	Nov
Price	£65	£75	£90	£110	£135	£95	£90	£75

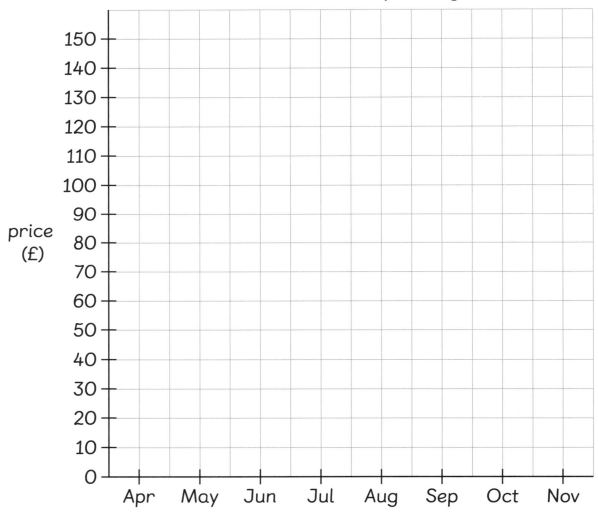

Price of a Holiday Cottage

(a) [   ] is the most expensive month.

(b) The largest monthly increase in price is between the month of

[   ] and the month of [   ].

(c) There is a difference of £ [   ] between the most expensive and the least expensive month.

(d) The largest monthly difference in price is between the month of [   ] and the month of [   ].

2 The table shows the average exchange rate from British pounds to Canadian dollars in a given year. When the exchange rate from British pounds to Canadian dollars is 1.67, it means that £1 would buy $1.67.

Year	2017	2018	2019	2020
Exchange rate	1.67	1.73	1.69	1.72

Draw a line graph using the information in the table.

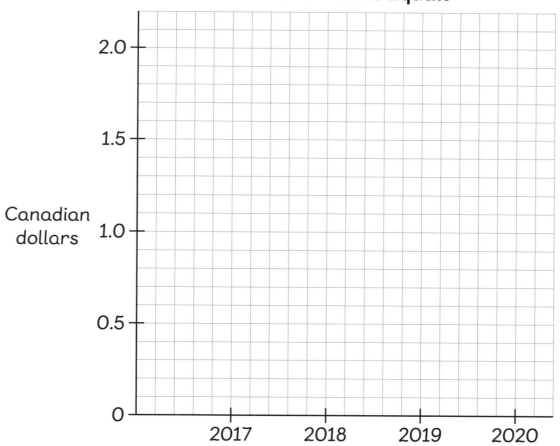

1 British Pound Equals

Telling time on a 24-hour clock

Starter

Emma is going to the cinema at 18:00.
What time is 18:00?

Example

My clock only goes to 12.

18:00

This clock shows 18:00. It is a 24-hour clock.

midnight   6:00 a.m.   noon   6:00 p.m.   midnight

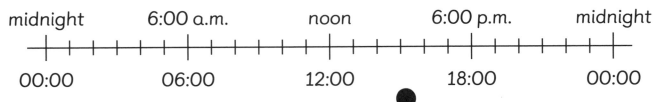

00:00   06:00   12:00   18:00   00:00

18:00 is how we show 6 p.m. on a 24-hour clock.
When using a 24-hour clock we write 6:00 p.m. as 18:00.

On a 24-hour clock 6:00 a.m. is shown as 06:00 and 6:00 p.m. is shown as 18:00.

1 Complete the table.

12-hour clock	24-hour clock
1:00 p.m.	
	14:30
3:15 p.m.	
	18:45
5:20 a.m.	
12 noon	
11:30 p.m.	
	00:00

2 This is a train timetable from London Bridge Railway Station to Brighton.

From: London To: Brighton		
Train	Depart	Arrive
Train A	15:15	16:17
Train B	15:45	16:47
Train C	16:05	17:13

(a) Amira wants to arrive in Brighton just before 5:00 p.m.

Which train should she take? _____

(b) How long does the 15:45 train take to get to Brighton? _____

Changing time in minutes to seconds

Starter

Holly skips for 5 and a half minutes. How many seconds are there in 5 and a half minutes?

Example

We need to multiply 60 by 5 to know how many seconds are in 5 minutes.

$60 \times 5 = 300$

One minute has 60 seconds. A half minute is 30 seconds.

We then need to add 300 and 30. $300 + 30 = 330$

I can use a number line to help me.

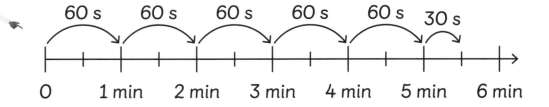

60 s	60 s	60 s	60 s	60 s	30 s

0   1 min   2 min   3 min   4 min   5 min   6 min

There are 330 seconds in 5 and a half minutes.

Practice

1 Fill in the blanks.

(a) 2 min = [ ] s

(b) [ ] min = 240 s

(c) 5 min = [ ] s

(d) [ ] min = 180 s

2 Ravi read his novel for 12 minutes and 40 seconds.
For how many seconds did he read in total?

Ravi read for [ ] seconds in total.

3 Draw lines to match.

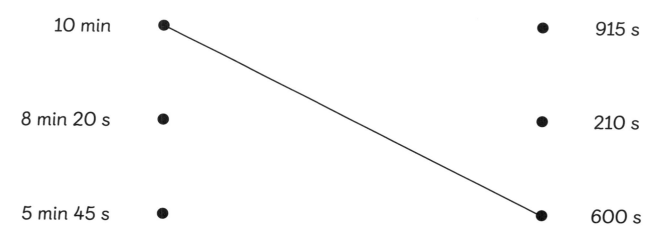

10 min   915 s

8 min 20 s   210 s

5 min 45 s   600 s

$3\frac{1}{2}$ min   500 s

15 min 15 s   345 s

Changing time in hours to minutes

Starter

Ruby was at a theme park for 4 hours and 45 minutes.
For how many minutes was she at the theme park?

Theme Park

Example

1 hour has 60 minutes.
We need to multiply 60 by 4 to work out how many minutes are in 4 hours.
$60 \times 4 = 240$

Next, we need to add 45 minutes to 240 minutes.
$240 + 45 = 285$

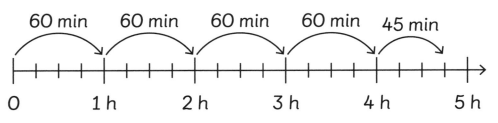

Ruby was at the theme park for 285 minutes.

1 Fill in the blanks.

(a) 3 h = ☐ min   (b) ☐ h = 300 min

(c) 7 h = ☐ min   (d) ☐ h = 660 min

2 The school day is 6 hours and 30 minutes.
How many minutes are there in 6 hours and 30 minutes?

☐

6 h 30 min = ☐ min

3 Match.

9 h ●   ● 732 min

8 h 45 min ●   ● 270 min

$4\frac{1}{2}$ h ●   ● 540 min

7 h 10 min ●   ● 525 min

12 h 12 min ●   ● 430 min

Solving problems on duration of time

Starter

Lulu's mum roasts a chicken for 90 minutes.
At what time will the chicken be ready if she begins roasting it at 11:45?

Example

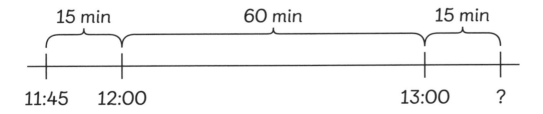

13:00 is 1 p.m.
13:15 is 1:15 p.m.

13:00 is 1 o'clock in the afternoon.

The chicken will be ready at 13:15.

1 Elliott puts a cake in the oven to bake at 10:45.
He takes the cake out of the oven after 45 minutes.
At what time does Elliott take the cake out of the oven?

| | min | | min |

10:45   11:00   [   ]

[   ]

Elliott takes the cake out of the oven at [   ] .

2 Holly got on a train at 16:45. She got off the train at 18:00.
How long was her train journey?

[   ]

New Cross Station

Holly's train journey was [   ] hour and [   ] minutes.

3 Ravi and his family need to arrive at the theatre at 18:30.
The journey from home takes 1 hour and 25 minutes.
At what time should they leave home?

[   ]

Ravi and his family should leave home at [   ] .

Changing years to months

Starter

Today is Sam's 8th birthday.
His younger brother is 6 years and 6 months old.
What are their ages in months?

Example

Sam is 8 years old.
There are 12 months in a year.
I can work out how many months
old Sam is like this.

1 year = 12 months
2 years = 24 months
4 years = 48 months
8 years = 96 months

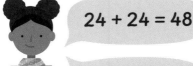

24 + 24 = 48

48 + 48 = 96

We can also just multiply.
8 × 12 = 96

Sam is 96 months old.

Sam's younger brother is 6 years and
6 months old. First we multiply to find how
many months there are in 6 years.

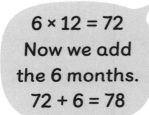

6 × 12 = 72
Now we add
the 6 months.
72 + 6 = 78

Sam's younger brother is 78 months old.

1 Fill in the blanks.

(a) 5 years = ☐ months

(b) ☐ years = 36 months

(c) 4 years 9 months = ☐ months

(d) ☐ years = 120 months

2 What is your age in months?

☐

I am ☐ months old.

3 Hannah is 18 months older than her cousin.
Her cousin is 88 months old.
How old is Hannah in years and months?

☐

Hannah is ☐ years and ☐ months old.

Writing amounts of money

Starter

How much money does
Holly have in her purse?

Example

Not all the coins are the same.
They have different values.

£1 has the same value
as ten 10p coins.

10p is one tenth of
a pound. We can write
10p as £0.10.

£1 has the same value
as two 50p coins.

50p has the same
value as five 10p coins.
We can write it
as £0.50.

 =

24

= £2.00

= £0.50

 = £0.30

Holly has two £1 coins, one 50p coin and three 10p coins.

We can add £2.00, £0.50 and £0.30. £2.00 + £0.50 + £0.30 = £2.80

Holly has £2.80 in her purse.

Practice

Write the amount of money shown.

1   　　　£

2   　　　£

3   　　　£

4   　　　£

Estimating amounts of money

Starter

Hannah has £30. She rounds the prices of these three items to the nearest £ to estimate the total cost.
Does Hannah have enough money to buy all the items?

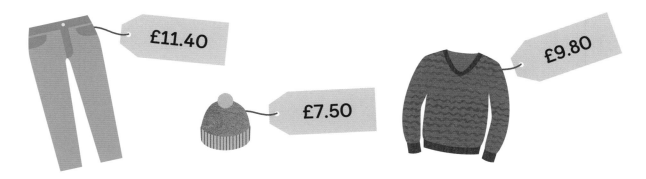

£11.40

£7.50

£9.80

Example

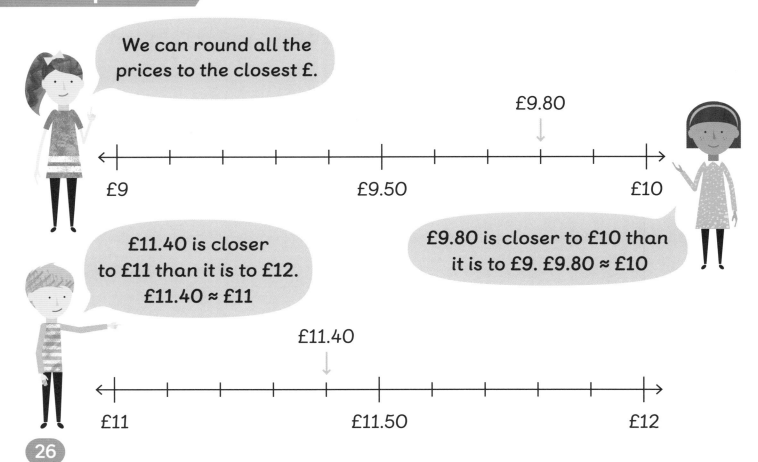

We can round all the prices to the closest £.

£9.80

£9 · £9.50 · £10

£9.80 is closer to £10 than it is to £9. £9.80 ≈ £10

£11.40 is closer to £11 than it is to £12. £11.40 ≈ £11

£11.40

£11 · £11.50 · £12

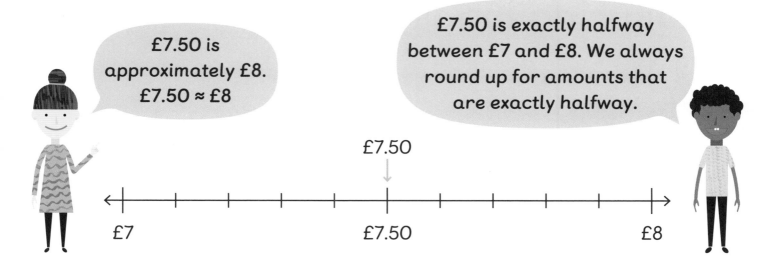

£7.50 is approximately £8.
£7.50 ≈ £8

£7.50 is exactly halfway between £7 and £8. We always round up for amounts that are exactly halfway.

£10 + £11 + £8 = £29

Hannah has enough money to buy all the items.

Practice

1 Estimate the total cost of the meal by rounding each item to the nearest £.

£3.75 ≈ £ ☐

£2.25 ≈ £ ☐

£2.50 ≈ £ ☐

Pete's Pasta House

VAT 929208510
55 – 56 High Street
Manchester UK M1
(161) 229-18345

Server : Charlotte
Dine in
Table : 62

Spaghetti Bolognese   £3.75
Garlic bread   £2.25
Ice cream   £2.50

Total Amount

The total cost of the meal is about £ ☐ .

Measuring mass

Starter

A pizzaiolo needs 5.6 kg of flour in order to make pizza dough for the following day.

I have 2 bags of flour with a mass of 2.27 kg and 3 bags with a mass of 454 g.

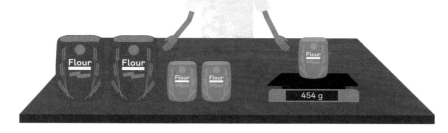

Does she have enough flour to make the pizza dough for the following day?

Example

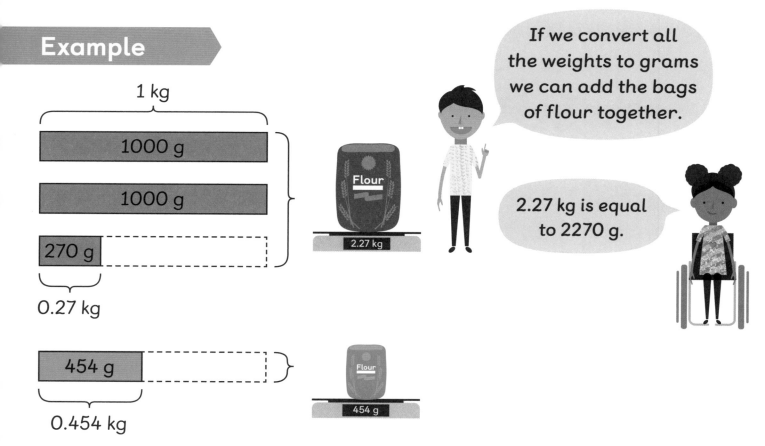

If we convert all the weights to grams we can add the bags of flour together.

2.27 kg is equal to 2270 g.

1 kg

| 1000 g |
| 1000 g |
| 270 g |

0.27 kg

2.27 kg

| 454 g |

0.454 kg

454 g

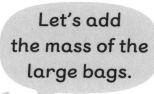

Let's add the mass of the large bags.

We can multiply to find the mass of the smaller bags.

$2270 + 2270 = 4540$ $454 × 3 = 1362$

$4540 + 1362 = 5902$

We can add to find the total mass of all the bags of flour.

5.6 kg is equal to 5600 g.

The pizzaiolo needs 5600 g of flour. She has 5902 g of flour.

She has enough flour to make the pizza dough for the following day.

Practice

Read the scales to find the mass of each item.

Put the items in order from lightest to heaviest.

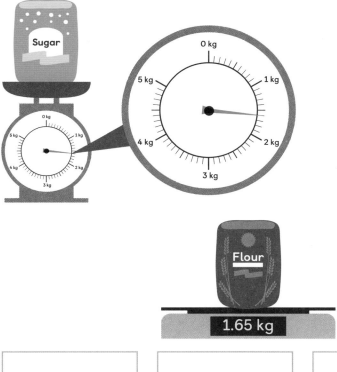

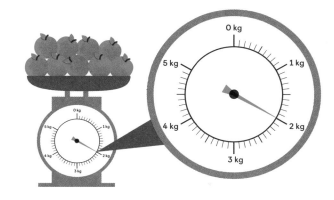

1 kg 95 g

1.65 kg

	,		,		,	

Converting units of mass

Starter

Jacob needs to post 2 parcels together. To post them together, the weight of the 2 parcels cannot be more than 3.5 kg. Can Jacob post the 2 parcels together?

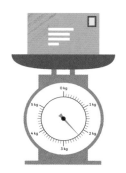

Example

We need to add the weights of the 2 parcels.

We can convert 2.3 kg to grams. 2.3 kg is equal to 2300 g.

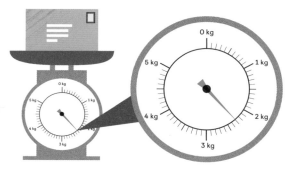

Now we can add. 2300 + 850 = 3150

```
   ¹2   3   0   0
+      8   5   0
───────────────
   3   1   5   0
```

1000 g = 1 kg, 100 g = 0.1 kg, 10 g = 0.01 kg, 1 g = 0.001 kg

1 kg

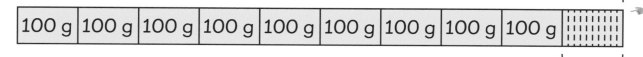

| 100 g | 100 g | 100 g | 100 g | 100 g | 100 g | 100 g | 100 g | 100 g | |

10 × 10 g

3.5 kg

1000 g	1000 g	1000 g	500 g

2300 g	850 g

3.15 kg

3150 g is equal to 3.15 kg.

3.15 kg is less than 3.5 kg.
Jacob can post the 2 parcels together.

Practice

1 Fill in the blanks.

(a) 2 kg = [ ] g

(b) [ ] kg = 2250 g

(c) 3.5 kg = [ ] g

(d) [ ] kg = 4050 g

(e) 6 kg 60 g = [ ] g

(f) [ ] kg = 10 000 g

2 Circle the lighter parcel.

2 kg 750 g

2075 g

3 Put these masses in order from heaviest to lightest.

3 kg 300 g   3.03 kg   3033 g

[ ] , [ ] , [ ]

Measuring volume

Starter

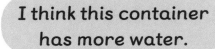

I think this container has more water.

I think this container has more water.

Who is correct?

Example

These containers have markings that tell us how much liquid is inside.

There are 5 steps between each litre on this container. Each mark is 0.2 l.

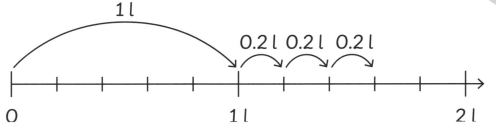

1 l

0.2 l 0.2 l 0.2 l

0   1 l   2 l

This container has 1.6 l of water in it.

There are 4 steps between each litre on this container. Each mark is 0.25 l.

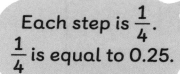

Each step is $\frac{1}{4}$.
$\frac{1}{4}$ is equal to 0.25.

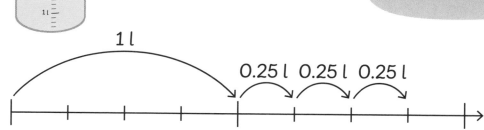

1 l

0.25 l 0.25 l 0.25 l

0   1 l   2 l

The shorter container has 1.75 l of water in it. 1.75 l > 1.6 l

Ravi is correct.
The shorter container has the most water.

Practice

What is the volume of liquid in each measuring beaker?

1
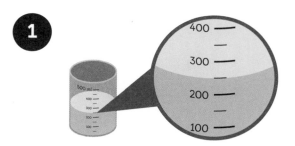

Volume of liquid = [ ] l

2
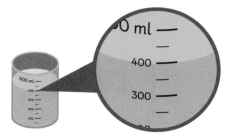

Volume of liquid = [ ] l

3
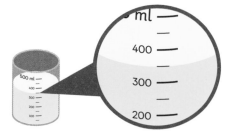

Volume of liquid = [ ] l

4
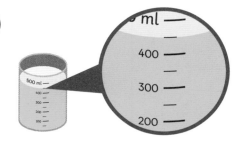

Volume of liquid = [ ] l

Converting units of volume

Starter

Which bottle has the greatest volume of liquid?

Example

1 l = 1000 ml

We can convert the volumes in litres to millilitres.

1.2 l = 1 l + 0.2 l
$\quad$ = 1000 ml + 200 ml
$\quad$ = 1200 ml

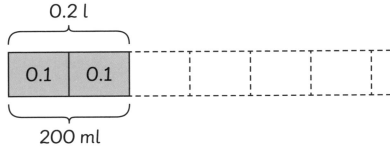

34

1 l 136 ml = 1000 ml + 136 ml
        = 1136 ml

950 ml

1200 ml is greater than both 1136 ml and 950 ml.
The bottle of orange juice has the greatest volume of liquid.

Practice

1 Fill in the blanks.

(a) 2 l = ☐ ml

(b) ☐ l = 1500 ml

(c) 2.25 l = ☐ ml

(d) ☐ l = 300 ml

(e) 4 l 400 ml = ☐ ml

(f) 7.07 l = ☐ ml

2 Put these volumes in order from smallest to greatest.

5.05 l   5500 ml   5 l and 5 ml

☐ , ☐ , ☐

Measuring height

Starter

How tall is Charles?

Example

Charles is taller than 1 m.
We need to use a measuring
tape to measure his height.

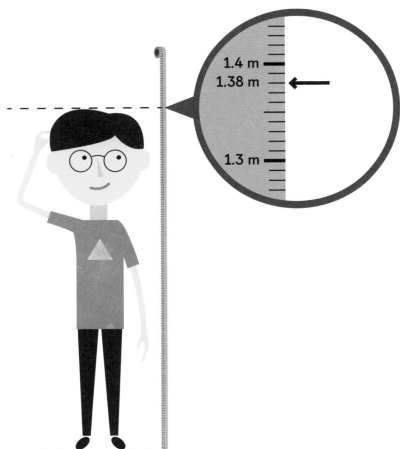

Charles is 1.38 m tall.

1 Find the height of each child.

(a)

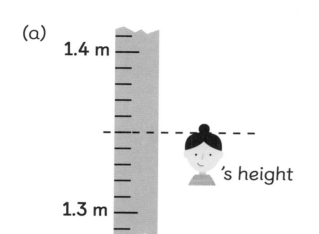

's height

[ ] m

(b)

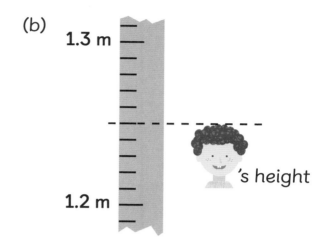

's height

[ ] m

(c)

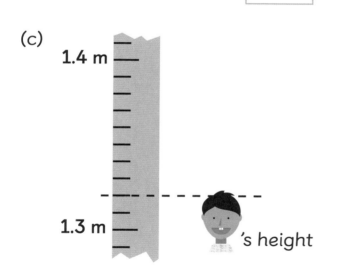

's height

[ ] m

(d)

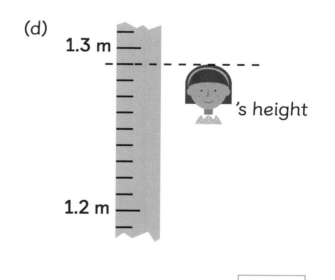

's height

[ ] m

(e) Put the heights in order from tallest to shortest.

[ ] m, [ ] m, [ ] m, [ ] m

Measuring length

Starter

Find the length of each side
of the picture frame.

Example

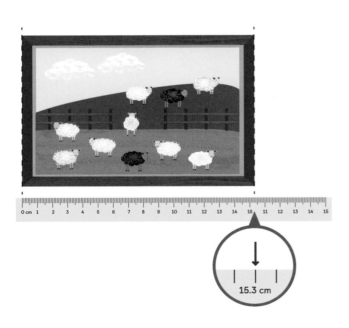

10.2 cm

15.3 cm

The sides of the picture frame have
lengths of 15.3 cm and 10.2 cm.

Can we use
this information to
find the perimeter
of the frame?

Use a ruler to measure the length of each side of these shapes.

1

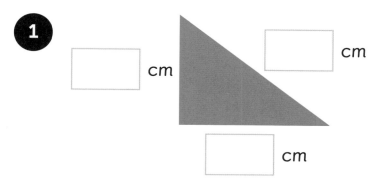

| cm

☐ cm

☐ cm

2

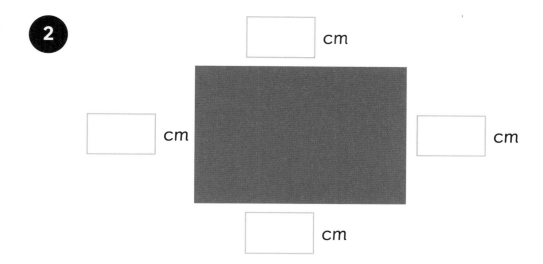

☐ cm

☐ cm

☐ cm

☐ cm

3

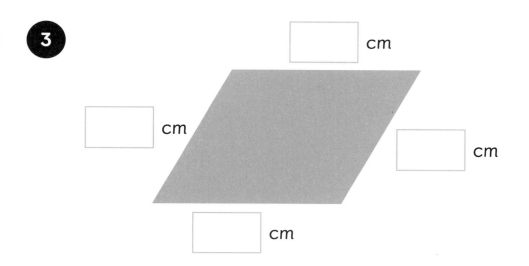

☐ cm

☐ cm

☐ cm

☐ cm

Converting kilometres to metres

Starter

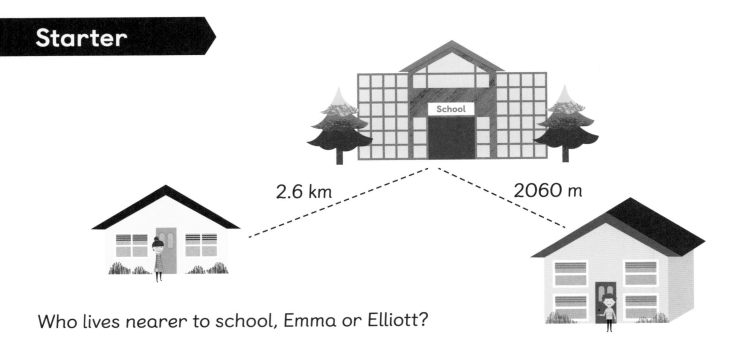

Who lives nearer to school, Emma or Elliott?

Example

Convert 2.6 km to metres.

1000 m

1 km

1 km

0.6 km

600 m

Emma lives 2.6 km from school. 2 km is equal to 2000 m.

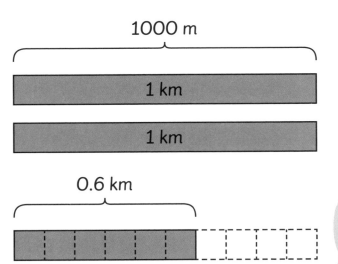
0.6 km is 6 tenths of 1000 m. It is equal to 600 m.

2.6 km is equal to 2600 m.

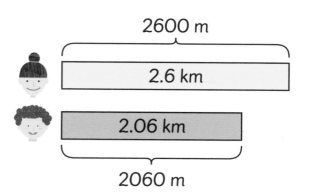

2600 m

2.6 km

2.06 km

2060 m

Emma lives 2600 m away from school.

Elliott lives 2060 m away from school.

Elliott lives nearer to school than Emma does.

Practice

1 Fill in the blanks.

(a) 5.2 km = [ ] m

(b) [ ] km = 1250 m

(c) 3 km 750 m = [ ] m

(d) 10.5 km = [ ] m

(e) 10.05 km = [ ] m

(f) [ ] km = 10 005 m

2 On Monday, Jacob walked 3.5 km. On Tuesday, he walked 2900 m.
On Wednesday, he walked 600 m further than he walked on Tuesday.
How far did Jacob walk over the three days in km?

Jacob walked [ ] km over the three days.

3 Put these distances in order from shortest to longest.

3950 m   3.9 km   3.899 km

[ ] , [ ] , [ ]

Review and challenge

1 (a) Draw a line graph using the information in the table below.

Day	1	2	3	4	5	6	7	8	9	10
°C	15	15	17	19	11	10	13	17	16	12

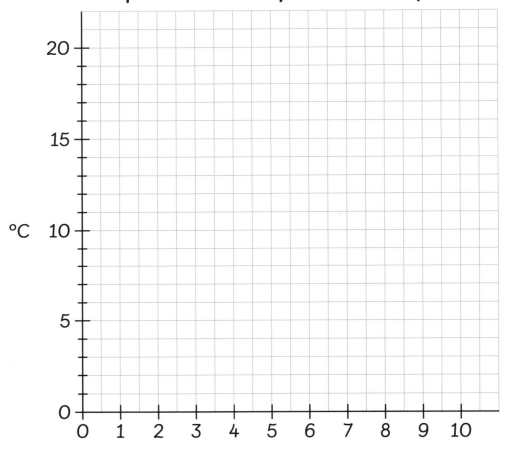

Temperature in a City Over a 10-Day Period

(b) The highest temperature was on day ☐ and the lowest temperature was on day ☐ .

(c) On how many days was the temperature below 15 °C? ☐

(d) What was the greatest decrease in temperature over two consecutive days? ☐ °C

2

£26.80

£23.25

£17.50

Estimate the total cost of these 3 items by rounding each amount:

(a) to the nearest £.

(b) to the nearest £10.

3 Sam is posting 3 parcels. The mass of the first parcel is shown. The second parcel is 500 g heavier than the first parcel. The third parcel is 0.25 kg lighter than the first parcel.
What is the total mass of the 3 parcels?

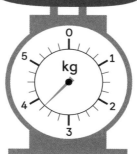

The total mass of the 3 parcels is [ ] kg.

4 (a) Ruby spent 35 minutes reading, then she spent $\frac{3}{4}$ of an hour playing football. If she started reading at 4:00 p.m., at what time did she finish playing football?

Ruby finished playing football at ☐ .

(b) Ruby went to sleep at 9:15 p.m. and woke up at 7:30 a.m.
For how long did she sleep?

Ruby slept for ☐ hours and ☐ minutes.

5 A train to London from Manchester leaves the station at 13:30.
The journey should take 125 minutes, but there is a delay of 35 minutes at Birmingham.
At what time does the train arrive in London?

The train arrives in London at ☐ .

6 Lulu has 2.5 l of orange juice in a jug.

(a) How many 300-ml glasses can she fill with the orange juice?

Lulu can fill ☐ 300-ml glasses with the orange juice.

(b) How much orange juice will be left over?

There will be [   ] ml of orange juice left over.

7 Find the volume of water in each measuring beaker.

(a)

Volume of water = [   ] l

(b)

Volume of water = [   ] l

(c)

Volume of water = [   ] l

(d)

Volume of water = [   ] l

8 Draw a square with 4.8 cm sides.

Answers

Page 5   **1** orange, mint choc-chip, strawberry, chocolate, vanilla   **2 (a)** 3 more children chose chocolate ice cream than chose strawberry ice cream.   **(b)** Two fewer children chose orange ice cream than chose strawberry ice cream.

Page 7   **1**

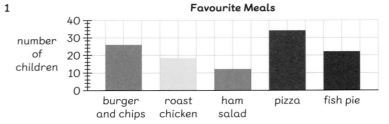

Among the group of children, pizza is the most popular meal and ham salad is the least popular meal.

Page 9   **1** October **2** July **3** 3 **4** 2 cm **5** 2 cm **6** September and November both had 6 cm of rainfall during the 7-month period.

Page 12   **1**

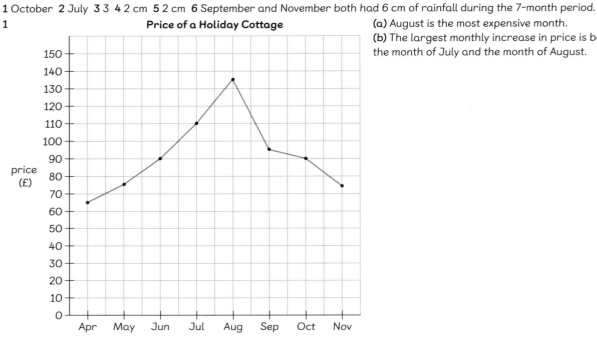

(a) August is the most expensive month.
(b) The largest monthly increase in price is between the month of July and the month of August.

Page 13   **(c)** There is a difference of £70 between the most expensive and the least expensive month. **(d)** The largest monthly difference in price is between the month of August and the month of September.

2

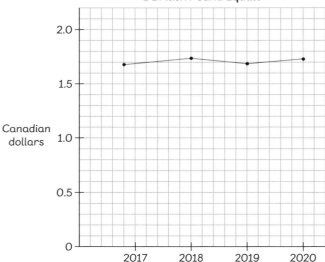

46

12-hour clock	24-hour clock
1:00 p.m.	13:00
2:30 p.m.	14:30
3:15 p.m.	15:15
6:45 p.m.	18:45
5:20 a.m.	05:20
12 noon	12:00
11:30 p.m.	23:30
12 midnight	00:00

2 (a) Train B (b) 1 h 2 min

Page 17   1 (a) 2 min = 120 s (b) 4 min = 240 s (c) 5 min = 300 s (d) 3 min = 180 s 2 Ravi read for 760 seconds in total.

3

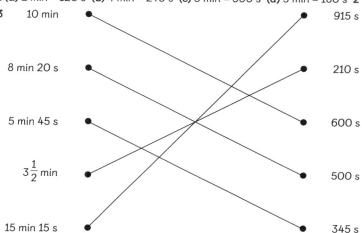

Page 19   1 (a) 3 h = 180 min (b) 5 h = 300 min (c) 7 h = 420 min (d) 11 h = 660 min 2 6 h 30 min = 390 min

3

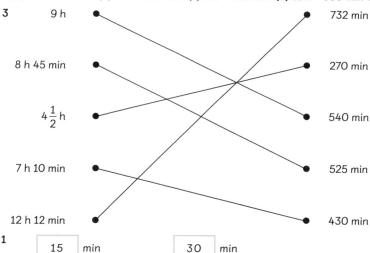

Page 21   1

Elliott takes the cake out of the oven at 11:30. 2 Holly's train journey was 1 hour and 15 minutes. 3 Ravi and his family should leave home at 17:05.

Page 23   1 (a) 5 years = 60 months (b) 3 years = 36 months (c) 4 years 9 months = 57 months (d) 10 years = 120 months 2 Answers will vary. 3 Hannah is 8 years and 10 months old.

Page 25   1 £1.80 2 £4.25 3 £4.40 4 £3

Page 27   1 £3.75 ≈ £4, £2.25 ≈ £2, £2.50 ≈ £3. The total cost of the meal is about £9.

Page 29   1 sugar, flour, pears, apples

Answers continued

Page 31   **1 (a)** 2 kg = 2000 g **(b)** 2.25 kg = 2250 g **(c)** 3.5 kg = 3500 g **(d)** 4.05 kg = 4050 g **(e)** 6 kg 60 g = 6060 g **(f)** 10 kg = 10 000 g

2    **3** 3 kg 300 g, 3033 g, 3.03 kg

Page 33   **1** 0.25 l   **2** 0.4 l   **3** 0.35 l   **4** 0.45 l

Page 35   **1 (a)** 2 l = 2000 ml **(b)** 1.5 l = 1500 ml **(c)** 2.25 l = 2250 ml **(d)** 0.3 l = 300 ml **(e)** 4 l 400 ml = 4400 ml **(f)** 7.07 l = 7070 ml
     2 5 l 5 ml, 5.05 l, 5500 ml

Page 37   **1 (a)** 1.35 m **(b)** 1.25 m **(c)** 1.32 m **(d)** 1.29 m **(e)** 1.35 m, 1.32 m, 1.29 m, 1.25 m

Page 39   **1**   **2**   **3**

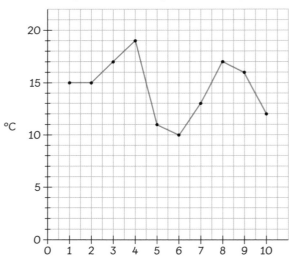

Page 41   **1 (a)** 5.2 km = 5200 m **(b)** 1.25 km = 1250 m **(c)** 3 km 750 m = 3750 m **(d)** 10.5 km = 10 500 m **(e)** 10.05 km = 10 050 m
     (f) 10.005 km = 10 005 m   **2** Jacob walked 9.9 km over the three days.   **3** 3.899 km, 3.9 km, 3950 m

Page 42   **1 (a)**

Temperature in a City Over a 10-Day Period

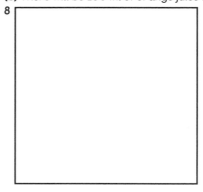

     (b) The highest temperature was on day 4 and the lowest temperature was on day 6. **(c)** 4 **(d)** 8 °C

Page 43   **2 (a)** £68 **(b)** £70   **3** The total mass of the 3 parcels is 11.5 kg.

Page 44   **4 (a)** Ruby finished playing football at 5:20 p.m. **(b)** Ruby slept for 10 hours and 15 minutes. **5** The train arrives in London at 16:10.
     6 (a) Lulu can fill 8 300-ml glasses with the orange juice.

Page 45   **(b)** There will be 100 ml of orange juice left over. **7 (a)** 0.55 l **(b)** 0.7 l **(c)** 0.95 l **(d)** 0.3 l

8